IMAGES OF
ST ANDREWS
PAST

A unique collection of almost 200
old and rare photographs (dating from
the 1840s right up to the 1980s) from
the collection of David Lyle who also
writes the illuminating captions.

This book is lovingly dedicated to my best friend and wife: Carol.

Text © David W Lyle 1997
Published early 1998

ISBN 0953211401

Printed by Terry Scanlon's
West Port Print & Design
14 Argyle Street
St Andrews
KY16 9BP

IMAGES OF ST ANDREWS PAST

CONTENTS

Acknowledgements

During the last ten years the David W Lyle Photographic Collection has benefited from the generosity of many individuals, but above all (indirectly) from George Michaelmass Cowie press photographer based in St Andrews between 1931 and 1982 - fully fifty years. The University Library, has many thousands of George Cowie's negatives, and to them I am grateful for their permission to use those photos's under their copyright.

Alex B Paterson had a fine collection of George Cowie prints and also a collection that George had collected of other photographer's work. I made many copies from Alex' collection thus adding to my own. Other sources for my photo collection include family photo albums of individuals and those from fellow collectors.

The photographs which illustrate the captions have been kindly lent to the author for this publication only. Permission to re-use them lies with the individual copyright holders and *not* with the author or the publishers of this book.

Many thanks also to: Mr R N Caddy; Cilla Jackson; Robert Smart; Alastair & Chris Radley; Gordon Christie; Walter Maronski; Helen Bee; George Gordon; Willie Paul; Willie Fulton; Gibby McMillan; Mabel and Kenneth Ness; Richard Govan; Gertrude Desborough; David Joy; and special thanks to Ian Copeland and his staff at the Hay-Fleming Library, Church Square, St Andrews.

Author's Introduction

John Menzies (1839-1905), my maternal great, great grandfather, came to St Andrews from Crieff to take up the position of Head Clerk at the newly opened railway station in 1887. In 1890 his wife was appointed as the caretaker-operator of the town's first telephone exchange which was situated in a room above Davy Grieve's tobacconist shop at 93 Market Street.

My Father, Gordon Lyle, came to live in St Andrews during the 1950s when he married Elizabeth Menzies and they set up their own newsagency and fancy-goods retail business in the shop of the late Trochie Fleming at 45 South Street.

I was born in my grandparents' home on the Lade Braes, was educated at Madras College, married a Cupar lass 23 years ago and we both continue to work in St Andrews where we have our home.

Images of St Andrews Past is a partial expression of some of the people, places, events, institutions and the moods of the town and its community during the last 150 years. Through photographs and captions I seek to recreate aspects of the community's latter history. Such local history undergirds the basis of modern St Andrews: both the people and their town.

So many inrrevocable changes have occurred within St Andrews during the period covered by this book that it seems worthwhile, I would say essential, to preserve the memory of that which has gone before, that which will never return, both for our own pleasure and for the benefit of future generations.

It is sobering to realise that elderly members of the community clearly remember the days when horsepower was, literally, the only means of road transport in the town. Even at the turn of the last century there remained abject poverty and squalid living conditions for too many of the populace, for Council Houses were not built before 1921 in St Andrews and the mass of private housing estates, built from the 1960s, were still under acres of farm land.

Shops were run by family concerns, often a rare bunch of characters, whilst the community of about 8,000 knew each other quite well. Tourists had started coming in large numbers in the 1850s, living in palatial hotels from where they would golf and putt, tour the mediaeval ruins, swim from the sands and delight in the uniqueness of this historic old town.

Within a life-span the character of St Andrews and its people has been transformed making this book of *Images* important, amongst all the other books about St Andrews, indeed it is imperative that both locals and our welcome tourists better appreciate our town's community history. I am pleased that a truly local author, a fifth generation St Andrean, has been enabled to record and recreate portions of former things; things which belong to the heritage of his own community which are brought out by these *Images of St Andrews Past.*

David W Lyle
12 St Nicholas Street
St Andrews
Fife

Events

Here we see newspaper reporter, Alex B Paterson, purchasing a ticket from Tommy Niven on the occasion of the very first St Andrews Town Service in 1951. The bus was driven between a stance outside the Holy Trinity Church in South Street and Lamond Drive amongst the Council house schemes.

Above is the scene when St Andrews first boasted a railway station in 1852. Provost Hugh Lyon Playfair opened the link from Leuchars Junction - he is seen here in the centre of the photograph with his top hat and large white whiskers. The situation of the first station was down by the Old Course near where the Jigger Inn is today, for the Inn was then the Station-master's House next to the 1st station.

The second railway station St Andrews was opened in 1887 and sat in a viaduct between Kinburn Park and City Park (a 19th century house) next to where the modern Bus Station is today. From 1887 until 1965 St Andrews was also connected to the Coast Line which took passengers down the cost to Anstruther and beyond.

The 1st passenger station became the Goods Station in 1887. Today the viaduct is partly filled in and the 1887 station platform lies under today's car park and roadway on the site. The final closure took place on January the 4th 1969 when the 11.07pm had arrived and the DMU quietly crept out never to return again.

This second photo is of the newer station on September the 4th, 1965 when the Coast Line was finally closed and St Andrews became a branch line again.

Cake Day in St Andrews. On the morning of each 31st December there was the annual Cake Day when local children toured round the local bakers' shops with the cry, "Ma feet's cauld, ma shoon's thin; gie's ma cakes and let me rin!" and were rewarded with bags of cakes.

The landing of early aeroplanes on the West Sands was a regular event for a few years from 1913. Pilots from Montrose (mostly) landed along the West Sands beach and taxied to re-fuel ready for the return journey. The garages of Duncan and Christie provided suitable fuel from the Bruce Embankment. Crowds used to go there to see the flying machines and their pilots.

The Light Brigade - 1901. This group of men worked for St Andrews' Gas Works which was situated between the harbour and the Abbey Wall beside the Royal George building. They are getting ready to join a procession through the streets.

Here we see a large crowd gathered in Market Place (part of Market Street) to hear the proclamation of the Coronation of George V on the 6th of May, 1935.

On the 17th December, 1955 the local Hunt met up outside Johnstone's Stables in Market Street and then flowed to the country via the West Port, seen here, at the west end of South Street.

This is the Princess Wilhelmina from Sweden languishing on the West Sands on September the 29th, 1912. She had been caught in a storm in St Andrews Bay. She had sent out a distress flare as she was being forced towards the rocks below the Castle. The lifeboat rescued her nine-man crew before the strong tide carried the empty vessel onto the West Sands.

This photograph would be taken at the beginning of the 1900s as a circus train comes to town up City Road to go down Bridge Street just past the West Port. Note that Tom Marr & Son had the bakers shop opposite and the building next door which was then a house and is now ladies and gents conveniences. The Circus would set up in a field near Southfield where Nelson Street is today.

This scene is set at the southermost part of St Andrews' inner harbour and the Lifeboat is being dragged ashore by volunteers before it was placed in the lifeboat house on the East Sands embankment. Note the gasworks chimney at the back of the Royal George building at the other end of the harbour.

The British Legion laid on a meal for the unemployed men of St Andrews. The event was held in the Victory Memorial hall in 1937 a time when there were still a great many unemployed.

Here we see George Bruce (centre) - Town Councillor, builder and poet - overseeing the work of land reclamation with four old fishing boats being filled with rubble, soil and cement. This extension, which preserved the tee area and part of the 1st fairway of the Old Course, was completed in the 1860s and was called The Bruce Embankment. For most of the 20th century two large putting greens were also situated on the reclaimed land. Today a car park and The British Golf Museum are sited where this photograph was taken.

1939 - This group of men on parade (outside Madras College, South Street) were the first to volunteer to serve in the Army. They were locals who were proud to do their duty. A number of these faces never returned to their native St Andrews.

The main Post Office in South Street was doing its best to avoid Hitler's bombs with a wall of sandbags around its entrance. Note here the giant Victorian iron flower pot of which there were a number in South Street at one time.

Telephonists at the main switchboard, situated just above the South Street Post Office, wearing 1938-issue gas masks at work. Sandbagging and gas masks may seem a trifle amusing to younger readers, but in the first stages of the War the threat of an enemy bombing and even an invasion was considered a serious and very real possibility.

Polish troops formed the garrison of St Andrews from 1940 until 1943. Here at the West Sands troops are busy digging to replace the large rectangular concrete blocks (which were made to prevent armoured invasion) along the length of the coast after an especially fierce tide had dislodged some. A few still remain visible along the West Sands today, between the road and the dunes.

Finally, in our brief look at St Andrews during the War we see another event occurring. It was the opening up of some town houses as Canteens for the servicemen. This canteen is at 60 South Street in a front room. Miss Irvine is serving a soldier. Note that a price list is in three languages including Polish.

This delightful photograph was taken one Sunday at the turn of this century in South Street. This was the site of the town's main Post Office from 1892 until 1907. The gathered crowd, in their "Sunday best", are awaiting 12.30pm when the Post Office would open its doors for an hour. There was a fee of 1d (an old penny) levied on customers who cared to pick up their own mail on a Sunday. Young men then wore plusfours whilst seniors sported bowler hats, caps and top hats. The women wore their square - shouldered dresses below the ankle, complemented by frilly and flowery hats. The building was better known during this century as the Christian Institute (now Innes' shop).

The St Andrews branch of the British Legion marches down the centre of South Street in 1933. This is a sight not seen any more, but between the Boer and 2nd wars the Legion were a very active organisation in the town. The event pictured here was the men parding for the funeral of Corporal John Ripley who was the only man living in St Andrews to have been awarded the Victoria Cross for conspicuous bravery in the battle-fields of France by the King in 1915. John Ripley was a self employed slater and window cleaner and ironically died as a result of injuries sustained falling off a tall ladder at Castlecliffe in 1933.

Here we have the formal opening day for the new Memorial Hospital in Abbey Walk on the 27th August, 1902. This photograph by Fairweather, the commercial photographer, shows guests entering the front door with the horse drawn ambulance standing outside.

This photo, taken in South Street in 1908, brings us the funeral cortege for (Old) Tom Morris: the famous greenkeeper, golfer and golf professional (to the Royal and Ancient Golf Club). Note (left) the restoration work on the Holy Trinity Church taking place then and (centre) the old Citizen Office at 107 South Street before its remodelling a few years after the funeral seen here.

1930s revellers meet together outside the Post Office in South Street as they join other locals at 11.54 on Auld Years Night. Before the New Year came in the pipes and drums led the gathered crowd in dancing and singing until midnight struck. They would then greet one another before going in two's and three's round the town to friends and families to celebrate the New Year. This event declined and ceased in the 1950s.

This photo of motor-cyclists racing along the West Sands was taken by George Cowie in 1950. The Scottish Motor Cycle speed racing had been held on the long beach since 1908, but this was the last year of it being held in St Andrews. In the distance the northern aspect of The Scores and St Salvator's Tower.

The annual event of the Kate Kennedy procession is one of the highlights of the University of St Andrews' year. It is also an event when locals, visitors and students mix in the crowded streets as the dressed-up students make their way from St Salvator's College, round the town centre and back. Here, as always, a student portraying Saint Andrew leads the procession (seen here) in North Street.

This photo depicts an early Charities Parade, here with pirates collecting money for charities at the summation of Charities Week. The Charities Week once culminated in a procession of floats in the town's streets (South Street here) followed by a fete held at Kinburn Park. The cessation of the parade came with the closure of Wilson's the soft drinks manufacturer in Argyle Street as it was always their fleet of lorries that were used each year.

Cows returning to Claybraes Farm (now the small housing estate known simply as Claybraes) being driven sedately up the lower part of Largo Road by the farmer's daughter in the early 1930s. The cows had been grazing in the grass next to Nelson Street.

This pier walk is a weekly event during the students term time. After the Sunday morning service at St Salvator's Chapel students come down the Kirk Hill and along the pier. This photo shows the outer harbour and the old tenements named inappropriately The Royal George (after a ship) with the gas work's chimney behind appearing to the left of the St Rule (Square) Tower.

18 year old David Mitchell of Brewsterwells Farm who, in 1932, was first in the Junior Class at the ploughing match held at St Andrews. David also won prizes for finishing, grooming and harness.

On the morning of May the first, 1950, the Madrigal Singers dance the eightsome reel near the end of the pier.

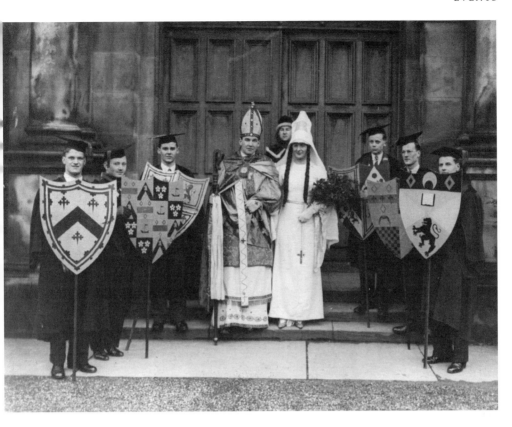

Bishop Kennedy and his niece Kate on the day of another Kate Kennedy procession which marks the arrival of Spring and is a toast to the young in spirit. The Kate Kennedy Club was an all male affair until recent years, but always Kate is played by a beardless 1st year student. Here they are pictured at St Salvator's College before the procession which took them in a carriage around the town centre.

Prime Minister Mr Balfour playing in as Captain of the Royal and Ancient Golf Club as Old Tom Morris applauds his drive. Note, back-right, the original Golf Hotel, then owned by D Mason and the almost complete Grand Hotel back-left.

A St Andrews' Merchants Association excursion by train to the Empire Exhibition at Bellahouston Park, Glasgow in 1938.

The 1930s opening of the Aviary (now demolished) in Kinburn Park. Clubmaker and cage-bird breeder Tom Auchterlonie persuaded the Town Council to provide it and it was there until the 1980s.

At the commencement of building the second Byre Theatre with the Crown Hotel in old Abbey Street in 1969. The Crown Hotel was once a coaching inn and dated back several centuries.

Ladies putting on a Sunday in September 1894. Note the Grand Hotel (Hamilton Hall) nearing completion in the background right.

In the late 1920s there was a revival of the Lammas Market dancing outside the City Hall (now library) with a band leading the proceedings. Especially note the head-gear of the ladies. Originally the Lammas Market dancing was done mainly by the farm workers who came for the feeing each August before it was moved to Cupar and another date.

An early Merry-go-round in Market Street (C. 1905) with Fairfield Stores and the Glasgow Drapery Warehouse which was on the corner of Church Street opposite Henderson the printers.

George Cowie took this view (over many years) of the Lammas Market in South Street, from atop the Boots building, seen here in 1937 outside the Town Hall which is opposite the Holy Trinity Church (left).

A glass of lemonade or ginger beer (and perhaps something stronger on occasion) at Old Daws refreshment counter at the 4th hole of the Old Course at the end of the 19th century. Old Daw himself had been a weaver to trade, then a ball maker and caddie later.

A Pierrots concert party at the Pierrot Pavillion by the Step Rock and the Bow Butts in August 1936. The first Pierrots of the previous century had played from tents on the West Sands before the Town Council built this Pavillion at the beginning of the 20th century. They stopped coming to St Andrews in the Summer shortly after the Second World War.

Girls at a West Sands bathing coach ready to brave the swell in 1933.

*The Coronation of 1937 and one of
MacArthur the Baker's Ford vans suitably
decorated for the occasion.*

Men curling at the rink beyond Law Mill in the Lade Braes.

Lined up here in St Andrews Town Hall are The Harmony Boys for their photocall before a concert organised by Mr & Mrs Bliss of the Pierrots in the 1930s. From left:- J K Wilson; Willie Menzies; John Kerr; Jimmy Harris and George Scott.

The Kinness burn floods Fleming Place (just off Bridge Street). Note the trees in the centre of Kinnessburn Road and the old gas lamp in the foreground.

The City of St Andrews Merryweather steam fire-engine (1901-1921) being taken through its paces on the Old Course with water being pumped from the Swilcan Burn one Sunday when there was no play on the course.

St Andrews' firemen with the new fire-engine of 1921. They were based and the machine housed in a building behind Holy Trinity Church in Church Square now conveniences for the public.

Billed as a Grand Tournament here are 'professional' players including Old Tom Morris and his son Tommy, Davy Park and James Anderson: all well known in their day.

This is when, in the 1930s, St Andrews had its own airfield. There were no buildings at the field but the local guide-book indicated that golfing gentlemen could come for a weekends golf in their flying machines. Here we see some enterprising person parked in Balgove Field during September 1938.

The legendary G M Cowie lens is this time within the University's Younger Graduation Hall in North Street at graduation time. Graduating with a degree is a the very heart of University Life and here a student is being 'capped' by Sir Malcolm Knox - notice too the beautifully ornate maces.

__Working People__

Two local stonemasons taking a break from their work. Jamie Spence and Bos'un Tamson were photographed by Thomas Roger circa 1892 in St Andrews.

A St Andrews Town Crier is seen here outside St Salvator's chapel and tower in North Street. He would play his drum to gain people's attention before he broadcast the news of the day to the listening townsfolk.

Mr Robert B Wilson, alias "Buff Wilson" was a newsagent, stationer and retailer of second hand golf clubs at 203 South Street. Buff was something of an enthusiast on golf having once been a professional player in Europe. He returned to his native St Andrews to open up his shop in 1927 which he ran until he died in 1947.

Jack Humphries in the once familiar auditorium of the "Old" cinema, in North Street by Muttoes Lane and the Police Station, in 1979 when the elder of our two cinemas was to close. Jack was the manager of the Cinema House for 50 years from 1929 until its sudden closure in December 1979.

Mr Willie Douglas was the Composing Room Foreman at W C Henderson and Son printers which were situated for over 100 years at the west corner of Church Street (where Bonkers is today). Willie started there in June 1927 and continued with Hendersons well after his official retirement in 1960.

Here are the St Andrews Railway Station staff of 1921: (Standing left - right) A Mitchell, Clerk; W Gordon, Goods Porter; T F Currie, Clerk; J Robb, Clerk; W Roberts, Signalman; J Proudfoot, Porter; T Anderson, Hoistman; (Sitting left -right) D Valentine, Chief Booking Clerk; J Docherty, Station Foreman; J Currie, Station Master; J Haddow, Station Foreman; J Crowe, Clerk; J H Thompson, Jr. Clerk.

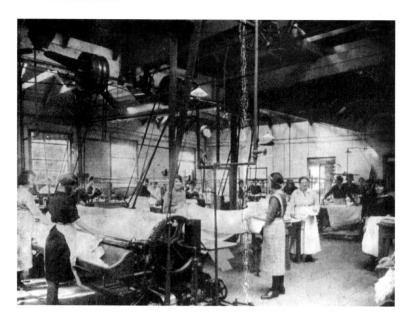

Some local women at work in the Ironing and Pressing Room at the Woodburn Laundry in Woodburn Place by the life-boat house. Many of the workers, especially the younger ones, were from St Andrews fishing community.

George Gordon (left) apprentice painter and decorator was brought up in a fisher family. However, he joined Messrs Robertson, once of South Street, and worked for them for over 50 years until the late 1970s. George is pictured here with Tam Dewar, a paint-mixer, in 1928 at the back garden of the shop.

Matt Richardson in St Andrews' first proper Pet Shop at the eastern corner of old Abbey Street at South Street where the RAF Association later had their rooms. Matt was well known for portraying a clown at the Step Rock Pool's swimming galas in the 1930s and '40s.

This is William Mackie with his horse and cart in the 1940s. Although he was a common sight in town he in fact walked in from Radernie and back again to sell his fruit and vegetables.

Local man George Thomson was a joiner to trade until the early 1980s. Here he is seen outside his small workshop (below) which was at one time a stable - the original cobbles remain under the floor-boards. Upstairs was his wood-store at 102 South Street. Although he styled himself as a joiner, he was also in fact an expert cabinet-maker wonderfully creating reproduction furniture.

Here is Willie Fulton standing in part of his yard off narrow Market Street. Willie was a slater and roughcaster who worked all around the St Andrews area. The business he ran latterly was "Black & Fulton" after Tom Black made him a partner, later leaving the whole business to Willie when he died. Willie retired in the late 1970s.

Workers inside the Forgan Golf Club makers where the Philips' Woollen Mill is today.

Here is James 'Bulger' Chisholm in 1938 in St Andrews. He organised the summer pony rides at the West Sands for many years, kept pigs and chickens, but was best known in town for his going around the housing schemes (he was semi-crippled) in his cart, drawn by Punch the pony, selling Sunday newspapers as well as the flowers of the season.

Local man Willie Paul worked for most of his life on the local railways. For some years he worked as a signalman at the Links Box. Here a driver and Willie exchange tablets to allow the 2.20 pm Dundee train into St Andrews.

Two railway Firemen and a Guard posing in the North Eastern Railway's Goods Station in St Andrews. They are seen in front and inside one of the larger goods trains earlier this century.

Here we see Alex Butters (b 1822) holding his clay pipe. By trade he had been a baker, but in 1893 he was appointed Castle Keeper of St Andrews Castle.

Here is Alastair Radley in early 1949 ploughing with two Clydesdales at the Canongate (now built up) opposite the Lade Braes.

Here are a group of GPO employees from the postmaster to the telegram boys. The town's post office was then (between 1892 & 1907) at 105 South Street (next to the Citizen Office, now Innes). The premises where purpose built for the Post Office but they became too cramped within 15 years and so they moved to the present Post Office building in the centre of South Street.

"The Daftie" is Willie Trail of St Andrews seen here in 1860s. He was a newsvendor in the town.

David Fenton began his working life as a fisherman based at St Andrews. When the local fishing became poor he went up the North-east to fish from there. He returned to St Andrews in 1921 to work for the Town Council. He is pictured here with the St Andrews Lifeboat of which he was Coxswain until its demise in 1939.

Here are some of the staff (and the coach) of the Cross Keys Hotel in Market Street in the 1870s.

Here are a team of bake-house bakers preparing the bread dough for the oven - the old fashioned way. The scene is set in John McArthur's bakery at the top of Abbey Street in the thirties.

This is Gibby MacMillan at work in his workshop at Bassaguard Industrial Estate. He was a local blacksmith (as was his father David (b.1892) and his grandfather - James - before him) for over 50 years in the town. Gibby also worked from 1948 until 1980 as a "retained" fireman. His business is continued by his son-in-law James Stewart.

George "Hackie" Hackerson, who was born in February of 1909 worked for many years as a message-boy for W C Henderson & Son of Church Street. It is true that some might say he was a bit simple in some respects but he was a unique character who had a pawky wit and was the kindest of men. His rare and dry sense of wit was tried out on everyone. One day he complained about the efficacy of his sweeping brush to Principal Sir Malcolm Knox who happened to be passing the shop door. "It's an awfy besom this ane" Hackie muttered, "First the heid cam aff, an' noo the haunle".

David Hay-Fleming (1849 - 1931) the local historian is seen here with his wife when they lived at Kinburn House (now the St Andrews Museum in Kinburn Park). He was a native of St Andrews and was known as an eminent historian, antiquary, critic and author.

Sir D'Arcy Thompson was a well known academic and he worked here as a professor at the University. He was both a humanist and a naturalist, a rare breed. He came here to work in 1917. He was popular with locals as he walked along the streets wearing white sandshoes, a large sombrero hat with a live parrot perched on his shoulder. He died in June of 1948.

George Cowie as a young man. George Cowie, a local freelance photographer for 50 years from 1931. He was considered by fellow press photographers throughout the Kingdom of Fife and beyond to be the most exceptional press photographer of his time.

At the end of his career, in 1981, he donated over 100,000 of his negatives to the University with the understanding that he would receive an honorary MA degree. The ceremony was to be in July 1982 but George died in April that year.

Andrew Govan Cowie was born in 1937. Son of George and Beatrice Cowie he naturally grew up in the aura of photography and soon learnt the basic techniques of both dark-room and taking fine pictures from his loving parents. In 1955 he left Madras College to work for the family business. His nature was more akin to his mothers preference for a quiet life. He occasionally assisted his father by *undertaking press photography, but the majority of his work lay in the photographic retail shop and processing rooms at 131 South Street. Andrew also preferred the medium of colour photography and took-on the colour work at weddings. Andrew was a very sensitive and meticulous photographer, never hurried, concerned with the artistic and technical refinements of producing prints and slides.*

The well kent gentleman, Church of Scotland minister, Charles Armour, when he was but a student at St Andrews. For a number of years he was first assistant and then, for many years, the minister of the Toon Kirk, the Holy Trinity Church in South Street. He is seen here with Rector Munro, accompanying him in a coach at a Kate Kennedy procession.

Alex Brown Paterson of St Andrews (1907 - 1989) was a local journalist to trade and reported on the area's news for 50 years. From 1931 he teamed up with George Cowie and they were not only great friends but also complemented each others skills. Alex was also the founder of the Byre Theatre which began in a renovated cow byre. Alex wrote for national as well as local papers. He also wrote many plays, sometimes directing also as well as being the Byre's upaid administrator for many years. Upon Alex' death fellow newspaperman, Tom Jarrett, wrote of him: "He was, without doubt, Mister St Andrews - the St Andrews citizen of the 20th century".

John Reid came from Dundee to St Andrews in 1896 when he worked for Judge Greig's drapery shop. John worked there for ten years before setting up his own business first in Market Street then at 47 South Street (now a vets). He was a Town Councillor for many years and was Provost of St Andrews from 1936 until 1942. John's daughter Meg Reid took over the business and ran it most successfully for many years.

Local man William Roger was employed as Keeper of St Andrews Castle in the 1840s.

Donald Mitchell (also known as Donald Blue). Although he was a very good golfer, maintaining a "scratch" handicap for most of his life he worked steadily as a caddy and instructor on the Links. Latterly he lived in the Model Lodging House in Baker Lane and was well liked for he was full of pawky sayings being an inimitable wit.

Tommy Polisher, seen here, advertising the St Andrews Flower Show on 23rd of August, 1888, seen here in Narrow Market Street. Tommy was a local worthy who was a little simple but he worked faithfully for Provost John MacGregor, doing any odd jobs required.

Here are the weather-beaten faces of three St Andrews fishermen from the mid-1900s. After the general exodus of the turn of the 19th century these three remained. On the left is W Chisholm who eventually became Harbourmaster. In the centre is Tam Black and on the right was "Bully" Tam Wilson who lived in North Street and later hired out rowing boats. His son was a fisherman as was his daughter also - unusual even today.

More traditionally (opposite) we see fisher-women working beside the Royal George building next to the harbour and they are baiting the lines.

This is Jimmy Alexander starter on the Old Course for 30 years since the Second World War. He was quite a character and he was a one armed golfer winning in international competitions of the day.

Davy Grieve was a Tobacconist at 93 Market Street. He was also a bird fancier winning many prizes for his birds. He married a local teacher and liked to go on holidays abroad, indeed he died on a cruise.

Born in St Andrews in 1868 Sandy Herd was a most natural putter and all his life was known as a tiger on the greens. He would deliver a crisp tap - with the clubhead kept low with his weight on his heels. He won most golfing honours but regularly failed to be more than the runner up at Opens.

Eric Auchterlonie and his father Tom in their Golf Place retail shop in 1955. They were established golf-club makers opening up first in 1919. Eric retired in 1986.

Old Tom Morris, greenkeeper and clubmaker and Professional to the Royal and Ancient Golf Club, in his younger days - a rare photograph.

Alan Robertson was a feathery ball maker in St Andrews and Tom Morris used to work with him when Tom was young. Alan Robertson has been styled as the world's first Professional Golfer - quickly followed by others such as Young Tommy Morris and so on. Robertson also invented the cleek - iron golf clubs made by local blacksmiths.

John and Elizabeth McArthur stand with family members outside the original McArthurs shop, bakery with a small cafe on the right as you entered at 34 South Street in the 1890s.

Gordon Lyle newsagent, tobacconist, seller of fancy goods, ice cream, postcards etc etc outside The Browserie at 45 South Street in untypical pose for he never smoked in his life. He ran his shop from 1955 for twenty five years into 1980. The shop is now owned by Donaldsons.

Old Daw Anderson is seen here selling ginger beer and lemonade (and perhaps something stronger to his friends) on the Old Course last century. Peter Anderson (no relation) quenches his thirst before playing on.

Born in 1860 Andra Kirkaldy learned to play golf on the St Andrews links - he spent more time on the golf course than at school. He became a professional golfer and a caddie. He was to follow Tom Morris as Pro to the R & A Club. Andra also caddied for members often expressing his opinions a little too freely at poorer players. He certainly was a character and a wit!

Two local worthies in St Andrews in the 1850s McKibben (left) and Gairdner (centre) with is daughter Josephine in narrow Market Street.

Two shop assistants serving a customer at the Stravithie Dairy at 158 South Street back in September 1986 when the dairy finally closed. The Stravithie (owned by Wallace then) was the last Dairy Shop in St Andrews town centre. Notice the 1 pint bottles of milk under the counter.

Born at the beginning of the 20th century James K Wilson (Just call me J K) was a stonemason to trade and had his own business in North Street at one point. Here he is seen in his yard, but he was also known as a popular off-the-cuff entertainer. He was also famously known as a personal friend of Bing Crosby: the American crooner.

1910 saw new regulations for St Andrews' caddies. Each one was asked to be "tidy in dress, sober when on duty and civil to his man". However these gentlemen would never have foreseen female caddies at St Andrews - an event of some seventy years later.

This is A W Keith at his chemists shop at 73 South Street. Formerly it had been the shop of chemist John Kirk. Some of the relics from this shop are housed in the St Andrews Preservation Museum in North Street.

Mario De Angelis during the '80s in his crammed pipe and tobacco shop at 207 South Street.

Here is an itinerant knife grinder in 1951 outside McArthur's bakery shop and cafe at 116 South Street.

Walter Fenton known as "The Pilot" for he was a seaman and lost his leg at the Battle of Trafalgar in 1805. He returned to his native St Andrews in 1809 to be with his family.

Dr John Thompson, later to be Rector of Madras College from 1955 until 1975, playing his chanter with (left) fellow student Roy Griffeth. They had their "bunk" with Biddy Rintoul at 48 North Street in the Winter of 1935.

Part One
The Old Town

The West Port during the Spring of 1947. Known locally as The Port, this entrance to South Street was built in 1589 and modelled on Edinburgh's Netherbow Port (not extant). This port was only one of a number of gates around St Andrews creating, along with high garden walls around the town, a non-military town boundary.

This photo, and the one previous, were from a series of Snow Series of pictures taken by George Cowie. Here we are looking at the West Port from South Street. Whilst Gibson House is just seen beyond The Port, Janetta's West End Cafe is seen next to T Christie the drapers as well as Neil Westwoods newsagency right beside the pedestrian entrance.

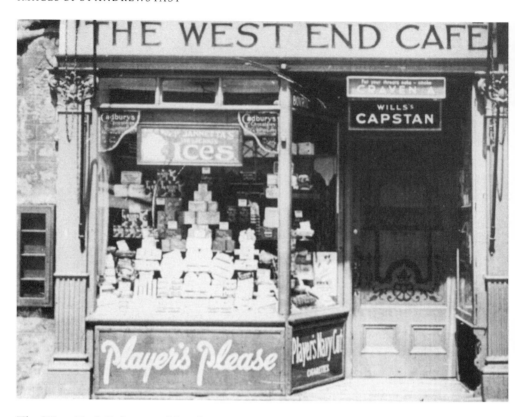

The West End Cafe owned by the Italian Janetta family who set up their shop and cafe at the beginning of the 1900s. The shop sold home-made ice cream, chocolates, sweets and cigarettes whilst the cafe was in the rear. At one time there were also billiard tables available elsewhere in the building. The premises is still in the family was latterly known as Jentries: an attractive bar.

A general view of the western end of South Street. Note the old cars of the period and the blinds emanating from many shops and, of course, there was much greater scope for parking outside the shop of your choice.

Here we have the very last gable end in South Street before Mr Suttie (in 1904) heightened the building and built a turreted round corner at the edge of Rose Lane next to the Baptist Church (which was refurbished in 1902 having first been built in 1842). Note Brown the Bootmaker next door (now the barbers).

Here we see very clearly the full width of South Street at its junction with Bell street and see the brave gentleman walking along the centre of the roadway. Note too the railings outside Madras College senior school with Aikman & Terras's shop to the left of the picture.

The old family grocer (the last in the town centre) of Aikman & Terras at 165 South Street on the corner of Bell Street in February 1977 when it finally closed down.

Here is part of the grounds in front of Madras College senior school in this very early photograph which takes in the Blackfriars Chapel (covered in ivy) with South Street beyond. The trees seen here were felled many years ago.

In this pre-1935 photo we see the Royal Hotel in South Street where today the University have Southgate at number 118. The Royal had its own garage with stately motor cars for hire although originally it was horse drawn cabs and coaches with their own stables.

This early photograph shows (left) The Holy Trinity Church and (right) the old Bank of Scotland opposite the new Town Hall in South Street. Note the condition of the roadway.

Part of old Logies Lane, including the City Arms pub and Hazel Rader the hairdressers, in July 1979. The buildings are being demolished to make way for the extension of Boots the Chemist of South Street. Note centre right the Tennants sign where the Star public Bar was.

This is the Holy Trinity Church of last century before the major renovation of 1906-1908. The building is quite changed and today the clock is in a central position upon the tower. To the left of the tower sits the City Hall which is the Town Library building.

Another view of the Holy Trinity Church but looking at its rear from Church Street before the 1906 renovation. Here Church Square is much wider and the church building comes right up to the pavement (left).

This rather dramatic picture shows the extent of the major 1905 - 1908 renovation of the Town Kirk or Holy Trinity Church in mid-South Street.

A view from the centre of South Street, but this time looking east towards the cathedral towers in the distance. Behind the trees stands (left) the Holy Trinity church and on the right stands the Town Hall with the untarred road and cobbles at each side.

The frontage of St Mary's College in the 1840s with a rounded extension which was pulled down by the reforming Provost Playfair.

This is Tom T Fordyce's second shop in South Street (the first shop being where the Alldays Store is today) Fordyce was not only a prominent businessman but also a Town Councillor and Provost.

The St Andrews Cooperative Society shop at 27 & 29 South Street. Today it is the site of Hoods DIY shop and was once the site of the Black Bull Inn until the 1840s.

This photo shows the edge of another McArthur's shop opposite the RAF Association premises at the top of old (and narrow) Abbey Street. The Association's building and Wilson's shop to the left of it were knocked down to make way for a wider Abbey Street in 1969.

This shop in the eastern portion of South Street was owned by David Johnstone and was established in 1950. Note the 1d Beechnut dispenser and the jars of loose sweets in the window. This building was demolished in 1969.

This is a much painted and photographed view of the very end of South Street with Queen Mary's house on the right and the Pends behind. We see the Cathedral towers and the Roundel at number one South Street.

Here is the Pends, built in the 14th century, and it was the main entrance to the Cathedral Priory. The Pends contained a series of high arches with a roadway below and the lodgings for its porter situated on the upper story. It is situated right at the very end of South Street.

109

*At the eastern tip of Narrow Market Street
lies South Castle Street which joins South
Street, North Street and Market Street. Its
junction with Market Street is where the
old gas lamp is in the picture. This part of
Castle Street was lived in by fisherfolk
families for generations.*

This wonderful old building was known as the Double Decker because of its double dormer windows. It sat at the junction of Market Street with Union Street and today the Buchanan Building belonging to the University sits in its place. The building was gutted by Fire in August 1934 and it was never again inhabited before it was demolished as unsafe by the Town Council.

This is a photo of Union Lane which ran behind the Double Decker from Market Street into North Street. It no longer exists.

Just beyond Union lane we view Market Street looking west towards the Whyte Melville memorial fountain (it has not operated as a fountain since last century) in 1898. On the right is the Temperance Hotel and John McGregors shop. Note the early electric light in the centre of the road.

Here we see a widened Church Street with J Cook & Son printers where later on would be W C Henderson Printers. Cook had a newsagency shop on the ground floor in Market Street. The old Holy Trinity stands at the end of Church Street (right) whilst (left) the building of the Glasgow Drapery store stands.

These very old houses stood where later the Glasgow Drapery Store stood (later Electricity Shop and now Global Videos) in Market Street at the corner of Church Street.

W C Henderson & Son Bookseller and Stationer to the University from 1886 until 1982.

Mr Niven and his son stand outside their butchers business in Church Street. He formerly had a shop in Market Street. The photo was taken in 1915.

115

*This unpublished photograph shows part
of north Market Street and the Town House
and jail in the 1850s. Note the ghostly
carriage and horse to the right in this early
calotype photograph.*

This is a view of the Old Town House, where the Town Council met and the jail in the centre of Market Street just off Market Square. It was demolished in 1862 after the new Town Hall (Queens Gardens) was built.

Here in Market Street we see something of the fullness of the Cross Keys hotel in the 1890s with an entrance (centre) to its stables. Today only the Keys public bar remains.

Market Square again looking past to the flower sellers at the fountain with horses taking a drink of water from it. Here we see the trees in Market Street which were taken down in the early 1930s when Woolworth came to town and insisted the trees outside there shop should go; so all the trees in Market Street were felled.

George Gordon's fish shop in Market Street in the 1930s at 59 Market Street when there were several fish shops in town including another Gordons at 10 Church Street.

Here we view the Star Hotel (opposite the Cross Keys) which is now ground floor shops with flats above. Mr Taylor of Strathkinness is selling flowers by the fountain. Market Street was still a two way street whereas today it is one way flowing east, away from us here. Note the cobbles that remain in the street.

Logies Lane, between Market Street and South Street (looking South) where now shops have their premises to the left and then the Star Hotel had its public bar.

Horse-people gathering just outside of Johnstone's Stables in Market Street in 1955.

Cobbled west end of Market Street with period cars and the shops that were there at the time.

George Armit the Baker's shop at 107 Market Street with his Model T Ford van which my grandfather drove for a while. Armit also had another shop in Church Street, where Fisher & Donaldson are today.

Just off west Market Street was the Victoria Cafe and here we see their Tea-Gardens in Bell Street opposite from Howie the toy shop. What a haven this place was for busy shoppers!

Gentleman and children at the east end of North Street looking west in 1887 on a misty day when St Salvator's Tower is barely visible in the distance.

This 1845 calotype photograph of fisherfolk in North Street underlines the crammed poverty they shared yet at the same time they had dignity. They were a people apart, a peculiar people in many ways, but it was their shared employment and community life that gave them hope.

Again we see some fishermen sitting outside a little further along North Street. The man on the left is baiting the lines ready for the next fishing trip. St Salvator's tower is seen in the distance.

Here we have the Younger Graduation Hall which belongs to the University but was donated by Lord and Lady Younger of Mount Melville when it was newly built in 1929 and opened by our present Queen Mother when she was HRH Princess of Wales.

c1860 view of the former episcopal church in North Street with a fuller view of St Salvator's just beyond. The Church was replaced by the present one in Queen Terrace in the 1860s and this building was sold to the Free Church congregation in Buckhaven. It was transported stone by stone by sea to its new home and the building is still in use today.

In the 1950s Lammas Market showmen's caravans parked in North Street by St Salvator's Chapel and Tower. This practise ceased many years ago.

This is part of old Union Street looking back onto North Street (from Market Street) with the conical-topped roundel opposite.

Here is an interesting view looking from atop St Salvator's Tower looking east towards the Cathedral. Note the houses below where later the Younger Hall was later built. This was after the episcopal church was removed but before All Saints Church was built. The photo was taken by Thomas Roger in 1876.

St Andrews Martyrs Free Church in North Street built in 1852. It has since been quite remodelled by local architects James Gillespie & Scott in 1929.

Here we see North Street from its west side with St Salvator's in the middle distance. Note the poor road surface and the gas lamps in the roadway.

This was the Old Cinema House which was purpose-built in 1913 as a Cinema House. Here we see the old building with Jack Humphries and some staff outside. The Cinema House closed its doors in 1979.

Further down, towards the end of west North Street lies the New Picture House, our second Cinema built in 1931. "The New" still continues today with cinema 1 & 2.

Part Two

The Old Town

We start The Old Town outwith the Town Centre in old Abbey Street. Here is the original Byre Theatre which was literally a theatre created from a cow byre in the 1930s. The entrance to the foyer was at the right corner and the tiny auditorium ran almost the length of the building. An old ships ladder took the actors up to the attic where there were two small dressing-rooms and a green room.

135

Here we see the second Byre Theatre building, or at least the entrance to it in 1970 when it was first opened. A renovated South Court is seen in the far background and the greenery has hardly had time to grow.

Here is the Crown Hotel in the 1950s in old Abbey Street east side which was to be completely demolished in 1969.

This Andrew Cowie photograph shows old Abbey Street in the 1960s before it was demolished to make way for a wider roadway and open space under grass. Here, Greenside Place meets Abbey Street and today Abbey Court sits on the left of our picture.

This 1846 Calotype shows Abbey Walk, with its turrets, leading into Abbey Street beyond. It is much the same view today except for the furthermost turret which has been moved back to widen the road. The house is Dauphin Hill built in 1786.

The old Toll House (now demolished) at the foot of Abbey Walk near Balfour Place. Behind the cottage the Abbey Wall runs past and up to the Tiends Yett: a gate into the priory.

Down in what is today called Woodburn Park by the Kinnessburn beyond Woodburn Terrace our picture shows a farm worker at work in the field where today children play and dogs go for "walkies". The chimney in the background belongs to the Woodburn Laundry.

Taken at the beginning of the 20th century this photograph shows that where the west end of St Nicholas Street is there was farmland. You can see the BB Hall centre-left and to its right the Bute Medical Building.

141

Here we see the Kinness Burn running along (this side) what is now Kinnessburn Road. Dempster Terrace opposite was built in the early 1890s and further up we see the Episcopal Church's pointed tower built in 1892 only to be demolished in 1938.

Looking from Kinnessburn Road we come to the entrance of Auldburn Farm where today we find small Auldburn Road and Auldburn Park: a scheme of Council Houses.

Queens Gardens in the 1870s with only a cart and horse coming down from South Street. Note the fine stonework above the doorways and windows and the dress of the youngsters.

The modern Shell garage in Bridge Street sits here where once David MacMillan had his smiddy and the Christies had their retail shop, cycle repairers and garage. Beyond is the Whey Pat.

An old view of St Andrews from a much younger Lade Braes.

Here is the old doocot with the buildings of Bogward Farm in 1906. Today the doocot is restored and is surrounded by modern private housing beside Doocot Road.

Here is an excellent view of Argyle Street. On the right is an 18th century house with crow stepped gable which was once next to Bull Ritchie's farm until it was built on after 1926. On the left are the sunshades of Pirie the shoe seller and mender which had formerly been the shop of John Frame the grocer and wine merchant at 43 Argyle Street. Just discernible is a Wilson's beer and lemonade lorry standing outside the Wilson's bottling factory. The west port is in the distance.

Here we are in City Road as it joins up to Bridge Street outside the West Port. The house on the right was owned by John Cole, a local stonemason, until Hamilton the Blacksmith had it and nearby his workshop. Today the site is a petrol station and the house demolished. Note the narrow left-hand pedestrian entrance of the Port and note how low the house to the left is compared with the next photo.

This picture shows the full height of 1 City Road with its turret. This was the site also of the Oriental Cafe which was owned by Tom Marr & Son.

Here is a photograph of part of St Andrews Railway Station in 1965 with a DMU waiting to go to Glasgow down the east coast line. The bus station is over to the right with Kinburn Park to our left.

Here at the front entrance to the former Railway Station a veteran car and other vehicles gather, waiting for a train to off-load its passengers. Note the Royal Hotel's horse-drawn cab.

Near to St Andrews Goods Station a small goods train passes the 16th Green of the "Old Course" in the 1920s, but everyone is engrossed in the game including the guard.

Beach-huts on wheels at the long and lovely West Sands with the town's outline behind.

ST ANDREWS FROM THE WEST SANDS.

The are by the West Sands as it will never be again. A modern car park is built on this site and just parking anywhere on the grass in not on today.

Bolger Chisholm and his donkeys at the West Sands with the 1854 Royal and Ancient Golf Club premises behind and to its right the Grand Hotel.

Here we see the R&A Clubhouse (1854) and to its right the cottages it started in where later the Grand Hotel (now Hamilton Hall) was built in 1895. We can see how near the sea was to coming right up to the first fairway of the Old Course until George Bruce reclaimed the land and made it safe from flood.

Admittedly this photograph is something of a well worn cliche with the Swilcan Bridge on the 18th fairway looking towards the Clubhouse and the Grand Hotel with the 1st tee and eighteenth green between. However it must be stated that the Royal and Ancient and the Old Course play a vital role in International Golf.

Here are a group of golfers arrived to play a game at the "Old" in their lovely motor which is parked on the Links road.

To the left of this picture the modern British Golf Museum (owned by the R&A) sits where once was a road, a shelter (built in 1926 now demolished) and a putting green (half of which is now gone). This is part of Elephant Rock Beach.

This is the busy Step Rock swimming pool area in the 1950s. The pool was approximately 300ft long by 200ft wide. The Step Rock was closed down in the 1970s due to dramatically falling attendances, people preferring the heated indoor pools elsewhere. Today the Sea-life Centre is situated here.

Part of the ruins of St Andrews Castle near East Scores during the 19th century.

This is a 1887 lantern slide of St Andrews Castle which was built over 700 years ago on the Bay's outmost cliff. Once a fortress now only a ruin. Note the gradual gradient of the banking to the sea shore below compared with today's cliffs.

Here we view the cross shaped cathedral of St Andrews. The building was started in 1159 although it wasn't until 1318 that it was sufficiently advanced to be consecrated and used. It ceased to be used after the Reformation and has deteriorated ever since.

Here is another view from the St Rule Tower (known locally as The Square Tower) overlooking the west end of the cathedral and on into the town centre.

A view from the pier with the Cathedral towers in the far distance. In between is part of the outer harbour with a yall sailing in.

Here is a view of the old St Andrews Gasworks situated between the Abbey Wall and the Harbour. The works were constructed in 1835 and lasted until February 1950 when gas making ceased after 125 years.

Here is a view of the inner harbour at St Andrews when there was clear evidence of many fishing boats whereas toady the boats are almost all pleasure boats. The Gas Works are behind on the left with the Royal George building to the right.

George Cowie views St Andrews through his lens with the Kinkell Caravan site, overlooking the Town, as it was in the 1950s.

D. & W. AUCHTERLONIE

The Premier Clubmakers.

AUCHTERLONIE CLUBS
are the aristocrats of
the Golf trade.

**In design, in workmanship and finish,
they stand alone.**

SPECIALITIES.

PATENT BALANCE PUTTER	7/6
PATENT APPROACH CLEEK	6/6
PATENT PUTTING CLEEK	6/6
PATENT PUSH-SHOT IRON	6/6

St. Andrews, N.B.

ANTIQUES

In Furniture,
Old Silver,
Old China,
Sheffield Plate,
Ivories,
Bric-a-Brac, etc.

The favour of a visit to inspect our collection of Curios, etc., is respectfully solicited.

Old Jewels remodelled or taken in exchange.

FOSTER'S ANTIQUE SALOON

——— (Patronised by Royalty), ———

6, BELL STREET, ST. ANDREWS.

Jewellery Establishment, next Post Office.

'Phone No. 80.

'Phone : 100.

FAMILY GROCERS
AND WINE MERCHANTS.

A. HAXTON & SON,
131, SOUTH STREET
—— (NEAR POST OFFICE), ——

is undoubtedly **the** Firm in St. Andrews for Best Value in High-class Groceries and Fresh Provisions.

Particulars of Furnished Houses and Apartments to Let will be gladly supplied free on stating requirements.

GRAND HOTEL,

ST. ANDREWS.

Occupies the finest position.

Extensive frontages to Sea and Links.

Overlooking the Home Green.

Most modern and best equipped.

Electric Light.   Electric Lift.

Post-Office letter box in Hotel.

Tel. No. 176.   Apply to the Manageress.